Shards

~ Live by your own sweat! ~

Bill Boudreau

Copyright©2021billboudreau

WJB Publishing
www.billboudreau.com

Contents

Author's Note

Several of the verses/poems in this book have appeared in my earlier publications.

***

Quotes:

"I am a fool. I try to be right in a wronged world."

"The greatest flaw of human beings is the ability to think—too often, it destroys them!"

"When broken, it's how you put yourself back together that defines who you are!"

Voice of the Poet

"I am the voice of the poet.
Behold!

You cannot hide, for I peel the
skin, expose raw flesh.
No attire can cover you, for I
disrobe you, show your nakedness.
No wrap can disguise you, for I
expose sensitive nerves, sting your
moral sores, reveal the rot behind
façades.
You may use another name, but I
erase aliases, tell all who you are.
Masks will not suffice, for I rip
them off, burn them, divulge your
decadence.
In a mirror, I see you before vain
makeup—expose your guilt.

I'm society's conscience."

The Internal (Eternal) Conflict

As my thoughts wander,
In the corridors of my mind,
Driven by the subconscious,
Id and Super-Ego at war
On the battlefield of the Ego
Each struggling to dominate,
Suppress the Libido,
Driven by primal forces,
And forever confront,
The learned social mores

Spirit of Hope

In the human soul
Resides a cosmos,
Let it radiate—
    Beyond this moment
    Beyond this soil
    Beyond this state
    Beyond this nation
    Beyond this earth
    Beyond this galaxy
    Beyond the reaches
    of the universe

Creating Poetry

On the beach in Saint Malo,
France, I saw a little girl pick a
grain of sand.
In a Nova Scotia, valley, I saw a
little girl pick a bloomed flower.
In a rose garden in Ottawa, Canada
I saw a little girl pick a rose petal.
In the *Hetriere* forest, I saw a little
girl pick a tree leaf.
In the inner city, U.S.A., I saw a
little girl share a piece of bread.
In the Rocky Mountains, I saw a
little girl reach for the clouds.
In Port Aransas, I met this little
girl and asked her—
> "Why do I see you all over the
> world? And why are you doing
> the things, you do?"

> She looked at me innocently,
> and answered, simply,
> "I am creating poetry."

Look What've Done

Look what we've done, on our
way to 2021.
Look what we've done, since
we've begun.

We've come from the trees, to
hunt with ease.
We've discovered fire and prayed
to gods higher.
We've killed our brothers, are we
any better?
We've killed our neighbors to fill a
hunger.

Look what we've done, on our
way to 2021.
Look what we've done, since
we've begun.

We kill others because they pray at
different altars.
We've stollen natives' spirit, for
profits.
We've come for their gold,
infected their souls.

Look what we've done, on our
way to 2021.
Look what we've done, since
we've begun.

With sword in hand, we've taken
lands.
In name of our god, we've killed
their gods.
We've spread lands with false
prophets hidden in religions.

Look what we've done, on our
way to 2021.
Look what we've done, since
we've begun.

Measurements

O, how good we are at precise
measurements!

We measure bombs in megatons.
We measure wars in deaths.
We measure a nation's strength in
weapons.

Ah but, how we ignore and lack
capacity to quantify compassion.

We measure corporate success
with dollar figures.
We measure fame with
commercial exposure.
We measure worth with monetary
data.

But we've yet to respond to the cry
of hunger.

We can measure distance to the
stars.
We can measure time in
microseconds.
We can measure distance in miles
and millimeters.

But we still do not understand
generosity.

We measure height in feet,
buildings in stories.
We measure snow, rain in inches
and feet.
We often measure best by size.

However, we do not try to
comprehend the pain in a child's
cry.

We have the finest machine that
can measure heart beats.
We can measure food in calories.
We measure business progress
with a chart.

But we've made little progress to
understand a broken heart.

We measure politicians with words
he or she speaks.
Greed is measured with material
possessions.
Preachers promise paradise by
donation amounts.

But we do not know how to
account and reward heartfelt
kindness!

Moments in Time

Light forced my eyes open.
I didn't know where I was.
I screamed for comfort.
Eagerly searched the nipple of
sustenance.
It came to me.
It nourished me. I felt secure.
I slept long periods of time.
In my cradle, I stayed alone.
I needed constant warmth and
assurance.
I satisfied my demands with cries.

Slowly, I became independent.
I took more risks.
I didn't see danger along the path.
Others cautioned me.
I didn't hear. I didn't see.
I moved on the straight road.
I couldn't see choices.

In my forward vision, there were
no other directions.
I was unprepared to witness the
thorny passage.
I was unready for the pathless
forest.
I didn't know I'd to make my way.

The search for love began.
Search for acceptance was to never
end.
Rebellious energy brewed deep
inside me. It tormented me.
I searched for alternate routes.
I saw none.
It frustrated me.
I felt forced to follow a narrow
corridor.
I felt I was between two tall
cement walls. They crowded,
limited my space.
It made me angry.
It was torture to contain the
tension.
At times, I felt I was going to
explode.
It had to come out from within me.

It hurt people.
It hurt me more than others.
I continued to live with it.
Now there're only fragments of it.
I look back.
I was a fool.
Am I still a fool?

I've learned much as I've walked
through the forest.
I'm about to be out of it.
What will I see when I come out?
When I step into that clearing.
I think about it more and more as I
approach my exit.

Here's what I've seen and thought
on my journey through the forest's
moments of time—

I've seen children play.
I've seen children cry.
I've seen children's begging eyes.
Why do we bring so many children
into this world?
Why do we neglect them so?
They're the foundation of the
future.

We kill their minds first.
Then we brutalize their bodies.
Millions are hungry all the time.
Their eyes search for love, for
acceptance.
They don't know where they
belong.
Their souls are homeless.
Their minds are afloat in the vast
emptiness we've created.
They don't know who loves them.
We don't teach them to love.
Ourselves, do we know what love
is?
Have we lost that virtue?
It's only a word spoken by poets
and lovers.
We speak of it at times for
moneymaking purposes.
We're great liars.
Maybe love doesn't exist?
Maybe love never existed?
Maybe it's only a word we created
to raise ourselves above animals.
If we do possess the virtue of love,
let's use it.

Let's not just talk about it.
Let's use it in deeds toward our
children— toward each other.

Among the tall, towering trees, I
see the horror.
I see the revulsion that resides
within us.
It's dark.
Long shadows on the earth.
I've walked the battlefield after the
battle.
What a horrible sight!
The mangled bodies.
The pools of blood.
I've seen faces with the last
grimace of death.
In the distance, I heard the screams
of hate.
The destruction goes on.
I continued to walk through the
forest.
I stepped over the body of a dead
child.
Her face hardened with the
stiffness of death.

"What did she see before her last
moment?"
Her eyes are wide open.
With tears on my cheeks, my heart
pounded like war drums,
I walked away.
The powerful forces of gods are
upon us.
I feel it all the time.
They're in control.
A massive force; overwhelming.
No individual can combat them.
The mass of individuals must
satisfy the gods.
They force feed us all.
They tell us what is right for us.
But it's for their own wealth.
They become more powerful at our
expense.
We're their puppets.
We're their host to feed on, their
prey.

American Hero

Wide shoulders, muscular arms.
Ammunition belt across a thick
chest.
Green tank shirt and camouflaged
pants.
He wears heavy combatant boots.
A grenades belt straps his waist.
His right hand holds an AR-16.
His left hand clinched in a fist, held
high.
With his darkened face, he's ready
for the kill.
He stands ten feet tall.

At the entrance of Wal-Mart
supermarket on a quarter inch
cardboard, little boys stop, and
admire the American Hero!

In-Between Worlds
(Life's Twilight)

Waves unfold like multilayered
rugs on sandy beach than recoil
onto themselves.

Seagulls, alert, wait for human
waste.
Sandpipers eat microscopic
organisms on wet sand left by
retreated water's edge.

Children ignorant of the ocean's
power, play in the water, drawn to
it, not knowing why.

Primal forces us toward our origin,
our roots, in an in-between world.

Where the ocean and the shore
meet, there is a crossroad, an
overlapping zone of life, a place of
decision, whether to be a marine,
or land-living thing.

But evolution will continue, some
will move up on the dry land,
others will go to be with the fish,

and still others will remain in this in-between world, to be picked and serve as food to birds and crabs and trampled on by beach lovers.

Sometimes, between birth and death, we find ourselves in an in-between world!

Frivolous Gab

One day, at a work meeting a couple of company Vice Presidents were in attendance, a few Directors, and many subordinates.

Frivolous gab was indirectly proportional!

Human Beings

Sometime ago, on TV, I saw a documentary "The Camps."
A few days later, I watched the documentary "The Longest Hatred."

No other species on earth is as cruel to each other as we are!

Should I be ashamed to call myself human?

The Final Race

As I get closer to the finish line,
I have learned to slow down.
In this race I am not in haste.
The only ribbon at the end is the one that ties flowers.

Is life the only race where the last to finish, wins?

Eyes of The Living

I look into the eyes of the living.
At times I see Dante's inferno.
Other times, the garden of Eden.
Most of the time, everything in-
between.

I'm shown the horrors of many
nations.

The child I cannot help.
The child who lost his mother.
The old man who bleeds, from war
wounds.
The family without a home.

All in the name of domination
of one power over another.

When I was a child
I dreamt of a wonderful world, a
fantasy world, where everything
was beautiful, pure, and good.
I believed it was there for me to
live in and enjoy.
Where is this world now?
Where did it go?

Did it ever exist?
Or was it only my childhood
innocence at play?
Why couldn't I have kept it?

Ah! the cruelty of life!
The cruelty of growing old.
The emergence of reality
through time.

Time leaves its mark on us as we
decay and fade into dust.

We're a passenger in a train,
looking out the window.
We see the horror and good.
We're afraid to stop, get off to
help.

Why?

We speak good words.
We claim we're the higher form of
life.
Are we?
Look at our behavior.
Listen to our words.
Do they match?

Happiness

You may have millions of dollars.
You may have all the smarts.
You may be showered with
flowers.
But it's what you feel in your
heart.

You may have professional
success.
You may be socially well known.
You may be materially blessed.
But it's how you feel when alone.

You may have many friends.
You may have academically
grown.
You may be well till the end.
But it's if you have a home.

You may go to church every
Sunday.
You may pray to God every day.
And be at peace with the one
above.
But it's if you have someone to
love.

You may give of yourself to
others.
You may have everything that's
new.
You may have survived bad
seasons.
But it's if you have someone
loving you!

Journey to That Other Shore

Go love one, swim the swells,
Of this vast blue-green sea.
There, you'll be among friends.
Join them in their freedom.
Let them guide you, along the
golden sunset trail, that leads to the
other shore.
And when you get there, light a
candle on the horizon.
Let it become a star.
Someday, we'll meet you there!

I'm

I'm a lonely prisoner,
captive in my prison.
I'm a selfish being,
afraid to be human.
I'm a frighten man,
lost in my confusion.
I'm a forgotten child,
looking for my mother.
I'm a lonely old man,
who needs a gentle hand.
I'm a homeless straggler,
in pain with cold and hunger.
I'm a tired cowboy,
searching to rest my horse.
I'm a wandering sailor,
waiting for the north wind.
I'm a broken man, who needs a
woman's hand.

I'm searching for my reason to be.
I'm reaching for the answer.
Will I ever find my season?

Continuum

Charged energy in an infinite void.
Suspended, no visible references.
Time, an unknown parameter.
In a turbulent and violent universe
where a moment is eternity.
Interactions of boundless forces.
Powerful opposites and attractions.
Mirror images in search of self.
Evolution of galaxies, stars, worlds
in a vastness, and infinite time ago
enormous space, a likely science.
Time not gauged as we know.
What became me began.

With time and a learned intellect,
I have acquired discovery powers,
to go dream, reach to all wonders.
Let my thoughts and vision seek,
infinite desires in time and space,
and take me to my own reach,
universe, eternity, my final place.
I have the resources of all time.
Endless space through open doors
To explore all reaches of my mind,
and beyond.

Great Creations

Earth creates with opposites.
Oceans balance mountains.
Fire offsets ice cold.
Forests oppose deserts.
Storms counter calm.
Days to find our way from nights.
Men find equal opposite with
woman.

And to appease world sufferings—
    Musicians create with sounds.
    And in poetry we find rhymes.
    Painters create with colors.
    Nature creates with Mothers!

Diseases

I keep away from people, who have
contagious diseases—
Egotism, greed, selfishness
self-conceit, inconsideration
compassionless, me-isum I-isum,
gluttony, power hungry.
A lot this going around these days.
One must be careful—is there a
condom for this?

Doors of Life

Doors of life lead to many rooms.
Sad to those who open just one.
Joy to those who open many for
they experience, learn, and grow,
discover that each door, brings
them into a room different than the
previous one.
Each room has its own beauty,
colors and light, its unique joys, and
sorrows.
Walls are filled with pictures of the
present, past and hints of the future.
It's like living many lives in one.
But these doors are locked!
And can only be opened with one
key that resides deep in the human
heart!

Crossroads

Where sky and ocean meet
Where shore and sea meet
Where night and day meet
Where fire and ice meet
Where love and hate meet
Where heaven and hell meet
Where mountains and deserts meet
Where two hearts meet
Where life and death meet
There are crossroads!

Is Honesty Possible?

Is honesty possible?
When you consider thoughts not
shared.
When you consider thoughts
realized.
Fantasies that reside deep in our
psyche.
The wonders of imagined erotic
adventures.
Not reveal secret passions of the
heart.
Killer hatred that rages behind
smiles.
Revenge that's carried as a heavy
baggage.
Honesty only seen in children.
Learn in youth, the art of
deception.
Must we all play the game to
survive?
When we meet, are you who I
think you are?
Or the one you want me to see?
Is the hand you extend, connected
to the heart?

Or just the detached arm of a
mannequin?
When I come to meet you again,
whom will I meet?
Will I see you, or someone else?
Will you let me see you?
Or will you be afraid to show me
the content in the space since we
last met?
I'd really like to know.
I've known you for so long.
When will I really know you?
Is honesty possible?

Combatants in Life

We are all combatants on the
battlefield of life.
We must fight many battles before
the final fall comes.
We all have had our share of broken
swords.
Laying on the ground next to
wounded warriors.

But we must uplift ourselves and go
on.
Walk with our heads high and ready
for the next battle.
Sometimes, we come out of battles
with a shining sword.
Holding it high in victory, running
fresh blood along the blade.

Eventually, even the great must fall
and new combatants emerge.
Rules of battle change as time goes
on.
Old warriors lose, fighting with
outdated weapons,
Defeated by more vibrant and
vigorous young warriors.

They fight with more modern weapons and techniques.
In time, the cycle repeats itself.
The young warriors become old warriors, and they in turn are defeated.by more youthful combatants with bigger and stronger swords.
Blood of the old, defeated combatants drip along the shining blade of the young victor's sword.

We are all combatants in life.

All living being have a turn on the battlefield of life.
Some will be defeated early.
Others fight to their last breath.
Some say, there are more battles beyond the earthly battlefield.

There are many who say, "No."
And many others say, "Yes."
The scriptures warn us: If we do not do your battles here on earth, you'll have to do them after.

Conversely, if we do our battles in this life, you'll receive your rewards after the final one on earth ends.

It's said it is much less effort to do our battles on this side.

Battlefield on the Other Side—we hear that if one waits until he or she gets to the other side, the battles and punishments are severe and long.

On the other side, and under certain conditions, the battlefield is endless, in other words, infinit.

Those who arrive at this stage are lost souls and do not win battles anymore, they have lost the big one. It is a battle after battle, on and on and on…forever.

It is said that those who are here are the ones who have not taken on any battles of their own, before arriving on the other side.

They have not earned their reward
kingdom and who have used gains
of other's battles while living in the
earthly battlefield!

Dreams

Dreams come uninvited,take
control of the night.
They know my fears, makes them
real.
I scream silence, run and stand still,
reach and can't touch.
I awake in cold sweat.

What is reality?

Chain of Life

Living things, linked, like in a
chain.
One's droppings, feast for another.
Decay of one, banquet for others.

Ecologically connected, like a
circle, a perfect balance.
Break the chain.
Life ceases!

Mind Sculptures

Ancient traditions limit thoughts.
Ways built on outdated theories.
Imaginary castles sit on old blocks.
Resistance to new ideas deeply
rooted insecurity.
In fear, we seek the flock.
Hold to old references a must.
Alone, we go amok.

The past, laws of metaphysics,
Re-enforced structured illusions.
Human games, exist as gimmicks.
Unknowingly, tricks intelligence.

In groups and worn-out rules, like
fence that contain cattle never
bring mind to bloom, restricted
visions, accepted annals.

Religions promise freedom with
absolute rights and wrongs.
On earth keep thoughts in prison
Those who know are forever gone.

Schools tell what to learn, books
written by community, not
applicable to universal society.
Knowledge acquired unearned.

Manmade social clubs of those
who think alike.
Mass collection of duds.
Together can be a might.

Governments rule by procedures.
Inanimate policies govern humans.
Feelings, emotions, not a consider.
Thinking people are intrusions.

Corporations in control of you.
Always being told what to do.
They say the good is for us.
Profits for owners a must.

Bonds of two people in marriage.
Strap the mind of liberal thinking.
Influence of other to manage.
For union of two gaining.
Awareness of social mores,
exert pressure on me and you,
to act in accord to the ways,
and not see or do something new.

Friendship in time we know,
obligations and expectations on us,
interruption of personality flow,
union, to be like other a thrust.

Bosses impose severe restrictions.
Superiority complex in motion.
Self-preservation, insecurity,
submission, contradiction of words
and actions.

In time ill health takes its toll.
From body's nerves the ind is told.
Brain's preoccupation, healing
uphold. Life continues,
unconscious the goal.

Upbringing ways of forefathers,
With change in our parents is
passed on to us with errors.
The belief it's for our diligence.

Fear of being alone and sober,
we've become a society of addicts,
cause we don't like the picture.
We poison our minds, self-
destruct.

The bonds and hierarchy of family
Imposes demands, expectations.
On our personal individuality
Never free from its persuasions

Teachers advocate their views.
To growing minds of youths.
By the students to be used.
Acceptance of beliefs in mute.

Priorities of needs with age
Will be in a state of change.
More thoughts and less actions
Some reach self-actualization.

Commercial media out of control
Self-discipline to block their goal.
Being conditioned, don't know it.
What we need constantly told.

Birth brings inherited orientation.
Heritage sculptured our formation.
No upbringing will eliminate,
What is in us deeply innate.

Our prejudices are blind spots.
Experience tells us what's bad.
In wars, generations gone mad!

Be Free

Be free of chains from the past.
Be free of living someone else's
rules.
Be free of other's expectations of
you.
Be free of feeling responsible for
other's moods.
Be free of fears of imaginary
threats.
Be free of chasing other people's
dreams.
Be free to give your love to
whomever you want.
Be free to dream and go after your
own rainbow!

Carriers of Good and Evil

We carry more evil than good.
In relays of generations,
We received them like batons,
And passed them on …

Ancient Beauty

Her eyes caress you.
Her voice massages you.
    A face, story of humankind.
    A stare tells evolution in
    darkest continent—white gods
    came.

    Herded by the sword.
    On ships to other shores.

    Servants to masters.

    Mixed with indigenous race.

    Freedom only in words.
    Ancestral blood joined.

    Circle of life.

A Confession to Come

In a confessional, kneeling, it'll be dark and cool.
A small window will slide open.
Against a faded-light background
a profile will appear.
Feeling insignificant, we'll say,
"Forgive me for I have sinned."
"Yes, my child" a strong, soft voice says.
"Forgive me for all who have suffered and died in your name.
Forgive me for the hatred and violence against those who are different than I.
Forgive me for my greed, and not sharing with the needy.
Forgive me for worship of material wealth.
Forgive me for destruction of your creation.
Forgive me for …
Forgive me for …

The confession will go on and on,
…severe penance forthcoming!

It

In my infancy and teens
It did not exist.

In my 20s and 30s
It happened only to others.

In my 40s and 50s
It was in the distance.

In my 60s and 70s
A faint shadow looming.

Now in my 80s,
It is much clearer.
I can almost touch it
with my extended hand.

They do not Know
(To my wife, Mother's Day, 1993)

They know not what they have.
You, as the Mother of the lot.
Those who take you for granted,
your time is limited.

When you're gone, they'll know.
Respect for you, will then grow.

And as the family wanders,
Searching for that focal center.
Which is given to us as Mother.

A family without a Mother.
Is a family without a rudder.
Like a ship adrift on the open sea,
no compass to guide the crew.

Age never outgrows her needs.
Her voice heard till our last breath.
At birth, through life till death.
Longing the comfort of her breasts.

Flame

How do you catch a flame without
getting burned?
From one who has learned the fine
art of flirtation.
Like a moth, one drawn to the
flame.
Seduced by her warmth, her blaze.
Only to get scorched.
How do you catch a flame without
getting burned?

Beggars at The Crossing

Between Mexico and the USA,
many cross the Rio Grande.
On a bridge between two lands,
beggars with outstretched hands.

Millions pass the beggars' hands.
Some drop money in their cans.
It makes the giver feel superior.
For he knows a different hunger.

In the ladder of the human race,
doesn't matter where we stand,
with no dirt on our pale faces,
we'll have an outstretched hand.

We're all going to be on a bridge,
over a big river to the other ridge.
At this crossing we're all beggars.
And there will only be one Giver!

Living Coffin

We don't need a box to be coffined.
From first breath we begin the construction the casket—Rules, mores imposed on us, become a more restrictive box.

In this coffin, constricted,
confined within invisible barriers.
A cubicle with thickening walls,
from inside as we go through life.

Coffin of life entraps us in social walls imprisoning ourselves, our dreams.
Each day adds a nail in the box of life.
In our final encloser, the spirit finds freedom.

Sad, we entrap ourselves long before being entombed!

Devil's Opportunity

His death shook every house's
foundation in the village.
Leaving a void for Satan.
Then Lucifer arrived in a white
starched collar and a black robe—
Lost innocence!

Experience the Love

An invisible aura that encircles a
special person. Peace on the face of
a mother nursing her child. An
inner charge as eyes meet, a touch
of fingertips. To awake in a naked
embrace, a gentle contact on the
lips. Trust and unconditional giving
without fear. Compassion without
passion of the flesh. Commitment
through suffering that has endured
time. Unconscious assumptions
without doubts.

A state of mind that elevates and
allows one to cope.

Ecstasy

Whether you're young or old
Whether you're rich or poor
Whether you're ugly or pretty
Whether you're fat or thin
True love is still ecstasy!

About the Author

Bill Boudreau is a French Acadian, born and reared in the small fishing village of Wedgeport, South-West Nova Scotia, Canada. He has lived in Montreal and Ottawa, Canada, Massachusetts, United States of America and now lives in Oklahoma City, Oklahoma, United States.

He's a graduate of the Montreal Technical Institute and earned a master's in business administration (MBA) at Oklahoma City University.

Starting in his middle age, and still active today, he sings vintage ballads and love songs with guitar accompaniment. He has written songs in French and English published in his book, *Mes Chasons*.

He's retired from a long career in computer software systems engineering and management where he earned numerous awards.

In senior years, now in his early eighties, he spends his time as a poet and prose/novel writer. He publishes his own work and for many other writers. He has written and published numerous books, articles, poems, short stories that may be viewed at a website he designed: www.billboudreau.com